New Eyes
Awakened Poems

Dawn James

New Eyes

Awakened Poems

Copyright © Publish and Promote / Dawn James

All rights reserved. No part of this book may be reproduced by any mechanical, photographic, or electronic process or in the form of phonographic recording; nor may it be stored in a retrieval system, transmitted, or otherwise copied for public or private use without the prior written permission of the publisher authorservices@publishandpromote.ca.

New Eyes: Awakened Poems

James, Dawn

ISBN 978-1-7387600-2-2 Hardcover
ISBN 978-1-7387600-1-5 eBook
ISBN 978-1-7387600-0-8 Audiobook

Edited by Christine Bode, Bodacious Copy
Cover Design by David Moratto
Interior Design by Perseus Design

PublishandPromote.ca

Note to the reader: *New Eyes: Awakened Poems* is a companion book to the author's afterlife story
Unveiled: Autobiography of an Awakened One.

The information is provided for entertainment and inspirational purposes only.

Printed and bound in Canada.

Dedication

*This book is dedicated to those who have awakened
and those who are realizing life is but a dream—a vacation.
Raise your frequency, allow your consciousness to rise,
then take another look and see this world with new eyes.*

Contents

Dedication	5
Weeping Willow	9
Inseparable	11
Hug Me with Your Words	13
The True King	15
Call Me Felicia	17
Mr. Green	19
Medicinal Use	23
Got the Munchies	27
Inner Demon	29
Saved by an Angel	31
Life in the Fast Lane	35
Tears of Joy	37
My Little Sage	39
The Rock	43
Busy Bee	45
The Magic Is Now	47
Hungry No More	49

New Eyes: Awakened Poems

Sun-Loving	51
Eagle Woman	53
Earth Keeper Promise	57
He Got It All Wrong	59
Tropical Invasion	63
Leaf Medicine	67
Witch Hand	69
Breakthrough	73
Genie, Save Me!	77
I Am Night	79
New Heart	81
Who This?	83
New Ears	85
New Eyes	87
Unseen World	91
Freedom	93
Other Works By Dawn	97
About Dawn	99

Weeping Willow

There was a weeping willow beside my house
I wonder what it would say if it could talk
Would it tell tales like a lion or a mouse
Would it whisper to a squirrel or a hawk
Of a little girl seeing crazy fights at home
Between two people who vowed marriage until death
Hiding under her bed, chanting Ohm
Excuse me for a moment as I catch my breath
Raising dust on violent memories makes me want to sneeze
I would shut myself in my room and pray to God, please
Please make the yelling STOP
Yet I never shed a teardrop
I knew that weeping willow
Was listening intently
So, I stood on the balcony
Touched its branches gently
Willow, weep for me
Weep for me

Personal Note and Reflections
Weeping Willow

I remind myself that there is no perfect job, no perfect partner, no perfect parents, and no perfect children. That reminder came to me in adulthood after I became a mother of three kids.

However, as a child, I witnessed situations that made no sense at that young age. Growing up as an only child with no siblings or close friends, I relied on confiding in what surrounded me—usually Nature.

I have always been drawn to willow trees. There is sadness; however, there is also strength. Call it resilience, as these trees can move and bend in the strongest winds without breaking.

Inseparable

Matching yellow raincoats and boots
Swapped each other's lunch every day
Passing notes back and forth in class
Double dutch, hopscotch, and other play
I would make a ruckus in class
If you got a detention
Throwing spitballs and airplanes
To get the teacher's attention
She thought she was punishing us
Schoolteacher was truly lame
More time together after school
Snow, sunshine, or rain
Didn't see you in class today
Walked to your house to check
Chicken pox! Off for two weeks?
Give me a hug; what the heck
We will just have it together
After all, we're best friends forever

Personal Note and Reflections
Inseparable

Memories of my first best friend in Grade 1. We were inseparable.

Hug Me with Your Words

Aren't you tired of lashing me with your tongue?
My heart feels like it has been stung!

Can't you see the scars in my aura
From your venomous citations?
It's deafening me, the loud echoes
Of your negative vibrations.

I am suffocating in your anger and hate –
Which you call self-expression.
I can't breathe. I can't breathe.
I need resuscitation.

Don't you know you are the key?
Don't you see you are the cure?
End this pain! Haven't you heard?
I need you to hug me with your words.

Personal Note and Reflections
Hug Me with Your Words

Throughout my childhood and adulthood, I have had a few people close to me who love to criticize. A few naysayers and cynics too. Sometimes I wish I had a recorder nearby to replay so they could hear their hurtful words. Everything we say creates a vibration which ripples out like water to listeners nearby. These negative vibrations impact our aura, thoughts and emotions. Hearing constant criticism translates into verbal abuse.

It took me decades to become comfortable confronting the critics and cynics. But, with years of practice, I can now begin my sentences with "I need..."

The True King

Could not see, could not talk
Could not hear, could not walk

Cry, why me? What's the point?
Must stay resilient; can't disappoint!

Dust yourself off, kiddo; chin up
God gave you life and a full cup

Of kindness, creativity and passion
Cling to that and make it in fashion

It's not about the physical; it's what you bring
Your gifts, skills and talents are the True King

Personal Note and Reflections
The True King

Despite the physical traumas I endured in my childhood, I had to learn the hard way that non-physical qualities would pave the way to overcoming my setbacks.

Call Me Felicia

My last year of high school
We moved from the burbs to the hood
Got mugged the first day in the bathroom
Girl gang thought I was too good

Drug dealers at recess
Recruiting the newbies
Ganja and toking wherever
Wannabe Bob Marleys

Loner alert! Buzz off
Changed my name to Felicia
Hiding out in the study hall
Like I got pox or alopecia

Church boy started chatting me up
Can I walk you home after school?
Sorry, I don't date men, lol
Barking up the wrong tree, you fool

Personal Note and Reflections
Call Me Felicia

I was terrified to move from the suburbs to a gang-banging hood, so I changed my name and tried hard to keep to myself for nine months during Grade 13.

Mr. Green

Mr. Green, you have known me since I was fourteen
When my parents divorced, you represented my mother
You treated me like a little sister; I thought of you as an older brother

Your kindness was appreciated
When you offered me employment
I made good pocket money
For a little enjoyment

But when I turned eighteen
Things started to change
You would ask me to work later
So I had to rearrange
My courses, transportation
And when to eat, not to mention…

You knew I needed the money to pay my rent
Mom was ill and could not work; this job was heaven sent
Then too many invitations to walk me to the bus stop
You started calling me sweetie and honey—what next, lollipop?

The last time I saw you, we shared an umbrella in the rain
Put your hand on my waist, leaning in for a kiss—this is insane!

'You are married with three kids . . .What the hell?!' I said
'Mr. Green, I quit; find another honey to bed!'

Personal Note and Reflections
Mr. Green

Was he a wolf in sheep's clothing, or did he become twisted in lust?

Either way, I had to leave that scene!

My lesson learned: people are not always as they seem.

Medicinal Use

Shy girl getting ready
For her first high school dance
Feeling nervous and anxious
'Cause she may find romance

What if she steps on his feet?
Her imagination runs wild
Took a sip of Bacardi
Nerves calm now; she stops and smiles

Highschool is torture
Too many teens with issues
Walking down the hall
Feeling sadness in their tissues

How can she stay focused?
She needs to pass her exams, shoot
Took a sip of rum and coke
Their emotional noise is now mute

Breakup first
Was her Golden Rule
Ditch him quick
Or look like a fool

Fell in love hard
With her best friend, Jay
Took a sip of 100 proof
Wrote, "Forgive me, I must stay away."

Personal Note and Reflections
Medicinal Use

It's not easy being empathic, wearing your heart on your sleeve. Throughout high school, I drank alcohol to help reduce the volume of other people's stuff and numb my pain.

Got the Munchies

Cravings have no remorse
Cravings have no regret
Junk food kept calling my name
But my waistline couldn't forget

At every gas station, they seduced me
Ignoring the security cameras completely
Pulling and clawing, they forced my hand to touch them
Pick me, pick me they yelled—it was utter mayhem.

Until one day, my Higher Self slapped me in the face
You are polluting your body with this shit; it's a disgrace
I fell to my knees and realized my addiction
To salt, fat, and sugar—what a contradiction

Hiding behind the guise of *I got the munchies*

Personal Note and Reflections
Got the Munchies

My new eyes showed me how to identify low (and no) frequency foods. I abstained from processed, chemical-laced, flavour-enhancing, artery-clogging foods for years as a result of awakening. Today 90 percent of what I eat is wholesome non-processed food, mainly farm-to-table fruits and vegetables.

Inner Demon

I watch the pitiful cracks in my skin from dry lips;
how I have yearned for a warm, wet kiss.
I want a pair of moist lips to soothe my pain;
a younger man, an older man—it's all the same.
Starving for a seductive touch;
a few minutes, an hour; I don't need much.

Hmm, the Sleeping Dragon is stirring now;
under my skin, blood vessels growing—Ow!
In my deepest darkest space,
I feel the demon's tail rub up and down.
And I can't help but cover my face;
my fantasies exposed all over the place.

Hmmm, sweet explosions of desires released;
my Inner Demon got his way—I am pleased.

Personal Note and Reflections
Inner Demon

You don't need a physical being with you to have an orgasm.

Sometimes it begins inside out, naturally. Enough said.

Saved by an Angel

Pay attention!
We are never too far away from thee
Tonight, you are waiting impatiently
To accompany your parents on a shopping spree

Wearing blue jeans, a white t-shirt and beige sandals
Dad exits first, then Mom grabs the front door handles
Dawn, are you coming downstairs; it's time to go
My lips move like a puppet on strings; I hear the word NO
No, I don't want to go
WTF, I've been waiting half an hour
Why did I say no? My intentions lost their power

My feet were glued to the floor until I heard our car drive away
Something or someone, up to no good, forced me to stay
Three hours passed, then I saw a red flashing light
The police knocked on our door; my chest got tight
They told me about a car accident
And I couldn't believe my ears

My parents were hurt and in the hospital
I bent over and burst into tears

As I sat in the back of the police cruiser
I looked around and began to understand
No seat belts in the back seat where I always sat
There must have been a Divine Plan
They kept me home tonight, out of harm's way
Angel intervention saved my life one August day

Personal Note and Reflections
Saved by an Angel

True story. One summer night, my parents went grocery shopping. Unfortunately, neither came home due to a severe car accident. I had survivor guilt for years and, to this day, could not tell them what caused me to stay home.

Life in the Fast Lane

The hunters and gatherers died
when they invented linear time.

Instead of the heavenly bodies guiding our way,
they invented that pesky clock—what a crime, I say.

Alarms and notifications could drive me over a cliff;
I have to do more in less time, my heart racing, back stiff.

Constantly worried, pressure rising, I will run out of time,
replying to 200 emails a day while drinking gin and lime.

Gotta make more to buy more, to store more—this is insane—
is it really worth it living life in the fast lane?

Personal Note and Reflections
Life in the Fast Lane

I started withdrawing from my day job when I realized how toxic and exhausting it had become. Working up to seventy hours a week, not living. I was a workaholic for sixteen years.

Tears of Joy

An eternity passed waiting for your arrival
Felt so excited and elated—a love revival
Imagining the curves of your face and the colour of your eyes
Would you sleep through the night, or would we hear cries?

Looked like I was having twins—what a riot
Forty weeks passed, and then it got quiet
Went to the doctor to see what was up
He said wait a week; I'm sure you will pop

Seven days later, no movement, no contraction
Did Zumba and Tai Chi but still no reaction
Had to break my water; my baby's way overdue
Please wake up, I prayed; *we need you!*
Four hours later, after tons of pushing
Little Jess arrived, as cute as a button

Personal Note and Reflections
Tears of Joy

Impatience and worry after the forty weeks had passed. But, then, tears of joy seeing my daughter at last.

My Little Sage

My little sage
Only nine years of age
Playing chess with grown men like a Master
Rubik's cube rearranged, one minute or faster

Always got me thinking with your questions:
Is God male or female?
Which is faster, sound or light?
How big is the tooth fairy?
Is anyone truly black or white?

Questions galore, and premonitions too, like when:
The morning you begged me to drive you to school
I repeatedly said no, take the bus, like a fool
Got to work; my cell phone's ringing nonstop
Told two school buses collided, and my jaw dropped

Second time in Canadian history, this happened
Two school buses were involved; one almost flattened

Got to the hospital lickety-split
Little sage said angels told him where to sit
He bent down just before the second bus hit
The driver missed the stop sign; what a twit

Little sage with Yoda posters
Across his bedroom wall
Had a toy lightsaber
Pretending to be Darth Maul
He announced, *I came to Earth too soon;*
Man is still obsessed with money, which is sure to ruin
any chance to live in harmony, end greed and rage
My little sage
Only nine years of age

Personal Note and Reflections
My Little Sage

Every child comes into a parent's life for a reason.

My youngest is also my wisest and oldest soul in the family (older than me!)

The Rock

You think I am dull and boring
Yet I never nap, am never snoring
Unseen eyes capturing the winds of time
As magnificent clouds drift by
I daydream the same as you
I feel the heaviness of life like you do

But I am timeless and ageless
Never chasing answers, gurus or sages
Be still with me now, hush, and pay attention
The calamity outside you does not need your reaction
Not to mention...
The meaningless noise you call conversation

Be still and stop chasing the clock
Center yourself, start observing life like a rock

Personal Note and Reflections
The Rock

New Eyes showed me I could be the actor, the director and the cameraman, all at the same time.

I like being a rock, an observer.

Busy Bee

I would rather be busy than bored
Can you imagine me knitting and scrubbing floors
And what about the brain drain from watching TV
Ditch the soap operas and reality shows; that's not for me

Every Monday started with a three-page to-do list in hand
Had to finish all by 5:00 p.m. as I waved my magic wand
Blood pressure rising, insomnia, no libido—it was chronic
Results-driven, Type A, tunnel vision—a workaholic

What was I chasing—title, status and money
Busy Bee, you got no hive, you got no honey

Personal Note and Reflections
Busy Bee

Sometimes we do what we are good at, and sometimes, we do what we are passionate about. I spent twenty years at the former and am now spending my sunset years at the latter. Today, I got the hive and the honey, doing what I love and loving what I do, and my heart says thank you.

The Magic Is Now

Never look back, darling; it distracts you from the now
Never look ahead, darling; it goes against the Tao
You know, and I know we cannot stop time
Stop wasting mental energy because it's a crime

You will only find resentment behind you
You will only find anxiety ahead
Free yourself; it's time for a breakthrough
Or forever become the living dead

Seize this moment with your clearest vision
Magnify your emotions with every decision
That feeling in your heart ignites the magic
Don't miss this present moment, for it would be tragic

Personal Note and Reflections
The Magic Is Now

When I woke up, I burned my weekly three page to-do list. Quit the day job.
Slow living and present moment awareness are priceless acts to practice. Give it a try!

Hungry No More

You captured me with promises of external delights
You bedazzled me, stroking my ego to new heights
More this, more that, baby, you can have it all
I was a fool feeding on your lies and deception
Like the emperor with no clothes or perception
Your dogma and subliminal messages soured in my belly
That gut-wrenching ache had me twisting and turning
I had to purge this from my being; my bowels were burning
I excreted in technicolour:
First brown, then green, then yellow and finally white
All that remained was bile—Lord, what a sight!
I had to hang myself out to dry in the sun
I started feeding on her majestic rainbow rays
They caressed my skin, penetrating my soul for days
A full-body orgasm. A new high.
Mmmm ... Hungry no more, am I.

Personal Note and Reflections
Hungry No More

When I lost my appetite and started to withdraw from this physical plane, my body started to naturally purge. So when my second life began, sungazing became my thing. I replaced one source of energy (food) with another (the Sun).

Sun-Loving

Although we are millions of miles apart
I still feel your warm caress

The songbirds announce your arrival in the east
While petals close, bidding you farewell in the west

You shower me with blessings from sunrise to sunset
Light, energy, food, heat, fuel and more, yet

You ask for nothing in return
The unconditional love of the Sun

Personal Note and Reflections
Sun-Loving

I am a proud sungazer. I am in awe of how much the Sun gives to all living things.

Eagle Woman

Tomorrow is the big day; I come out of the spiritual closet
Speaking in front of hundreds, wearing my hematite anklet
Talking about how to raise your vibration
At the largest holistic expo in the nation

It's getting late, and I still cannot fall asleep
What was I thinking – time to find a bridge and leap
Yes, I am petrified my mind may go blank, and I get stage fright
Staring at the ceiling for hours until she appears in golden light

A vision of a woman with jet black hair,
Braided in two plaits, among the trees
She was calling out in her Indigenous tongue,
Chanting a mesmerizing symphony

Is she Algonquin, Iroquois, Blackfoot or Cree?
I touched my face and felt her skin—oh my God, she is me!
I heard the words clearly now, evoking something from the sky
I looked up and saw two large wings swoop by

It was bigger than a plane; how could this be
A huge brown eagle was flying toward me
It flew into the center of my chest,
And with it came feelings of courage and faith
In that moment, my fears and doubts melted,
And I knew I was in the right place

My new life as a public speaker had begun;
It was time to turn the page
I thanked Eagle Woman, she smiled,
And the next day, she joined me on stage.

Personal Note and Reflections
Eagle Woman

I had insomnia the night before I spoke on stage at the 2010 Whole Life Expo in Ontario, Canada. Eagle Woman accompanied me. I met hundreds of people and sold 400 books in three days at the expo. After that event, I continued to speak across North America and, eventually, internationally.

Earth Keeper Promise

How we treat the Earth is a reflection of how we treat our bodies;

the condition of the Water reflects the condition of our blood.

What we put in the Air is returned to us in a breath, and

when we shun the Light of the heavenly bodies,

our Spirit becomes entrapped in a calcified shell.

Take heed and reflect on these things.

They are gentle reminders of a promise you made long ago.

Remember your promise to protect, care for and cherish this planet.

Remember your promise to live in harmony with Nature and all living things.

Remember your promise to give as you receive,

and, above all, remember your promise to be an Earth keeper.

Personal Note and Reflections
Earth Keeper Promise

I channelled this prose in 2014 from a spirit guide, a male Ojibway Elder. He accompanied me in my office for months while I wrote my second book, How to Raise the Vibration around You: Volume I: Working with the 4 Elements to Create Healthy and Harmonious Living Spaces.

He also inspired me to write the poem Sun-Loving. He is with me now as I write New Eyes: Awakened Poems.

He Got It All Wrong

Airports shut down
No one home but you and me
Tried Om meditation
Screw this; I started watching TV
Binge-watching until the sun arose
Feasting on ice cream and chips, here goes
Twenty pounds from pandemic isolation
Driving restrictions and mental depression

No more separate quarters
You now lay beside me
Inch by inch, you got closer
Knew I needed company
I stared into your brown eyes
To ease my pain
Your confident stance
Made me feel safe and sane

We started taking long walks
An occasional kiss
You gave me friendship, laughter
And lots of bliss
Lonely no more with my male Titan
While hubby is stuck in Hong Kong
His dog became *my best friend*
He got it all wrong

Personal Note and Reflections
He Got It All Wrong

Airport closures forced hubby and me to be on different continents for almost a year. Our dog Titan went from being his best friend to mine as we bonded during the pandemic.

Tropical Invasion

There is a four-lane highway
across our yard;
two lanes up, two lanes down,
covered with Swiss chard!

We planted a garden months ago,
but no fruits or vegetables grew;
they took the leaves from every plant—
guava, starfruit, and even cashew.

Got a flashlight one night
and followed their trail;
found their Mother Ship,
Home Base, and Holy Grail!

Not going to let three million ants
come between me and my plants;
no peaceful talks or negotiations,
just silent ruthless annihilation.

Perhaps I went too far.
Who is to say?
Had them swimming in seawater
like a stingray.
Their camp was flooded,
leaf cutters no more,
tubers and vines started thriving—
tropical invasion became folklore.

Personal Note and Reflections
Tropical Invasion

Had a little outdoor drama adjusting to tropical living.

Took me a year to make peace and leave insects at peace outside.

Leaf Medicine

Eat from every tree save one
How could we be so ignorant?
Medicine cabinet is in the forest
Skip body wash, perfume, and deodorant!

Cancer-causing agents—hormone disruptors are the recipe
For man-made products borne of greed and devilry
Don't let Man change your DNA or pedigree
Return to Mother Earth's lush greenery

Soursop leaves shrinking tumours
Polyphenol in banana leaf for Parkinson's
Guava leaf helps with acne, manages blood sugar
And also improves your vision

The medicine in the leaf is stronger than the fruit
It's been proven time and time again
The Sun feeds it Chi energy
That's how it became Leaf Medicine

Personal Note and Reflections
Leaf Medicine

I met a medicine woman who treats people diagnosed with cancer. She showed me her garden and explained the cellular benefits of the leaves of certain plants.

Witch Hand

Isn't it ironic, you toting a bible, praying to God every day
Yet punishing your innocent baby girl, you think went astray

What was her affliction
Wanting to live without restriction?
Holding a crayon, cup or rattle
Always turned into a battle
Of beliefs, you swallowed poured by nuns
To be Godly, humble, repent, no guns

My only crime was using my left hand
You thought I was a witch, so you had to band
My left hand in a bag wrapped with twine
Fifty years later, I can still see the black line
On my left wrist; you crazy fool
Left-handers have creative minds; that is the rule

I escaped your prison by age nine at the bench
Played piano for hours daily—oh, sweet revenge

Receiving rewards, trophies and accolades
Using both hands, playing classical and serenades
Then you turned proud, *witch hand* became obsolete
Self-acceptance was my goal, and now I am complete.

Personal Note and Reflections
Witch Hand

Reminiscing of the battle of beliefs—about left-handed people. One goal of life is to love and accept yourself unconditionally and fully.

Breakthrough

Sitting under a red maple tree
A cool breeze blowing through my hair
Daughter's sixteenth birthday party
How I wished you were there

You missed so many memories
What a shame, but that was all your doing
Broke my heart and betrayed me
Never saw my babes smiling or cooing

Gave you my money; gave you my love
Bought you a house at age nineteen
I got married and was having a baby
With a knife you attacked me—violence unforeseen

Gave you no drama; never cursed, no lies
Why attack me, Mama? See the trauma in my eyes?

Read *The Four Agreements* and slowly started to heal
Stopped taking things personally and broke this family ordeal

Mama, your anger got the best of you
I still feel your love, though. . .major breakthrough

Personal Note and Reflections
Breakthrough

How do you forgive someone who tried to end your life?

It took me sixteen years and many tears to realize it was not about me but my mother's issue.

Genie, Save Me!

Your patience astounds me; it's amazing

8,000 years you waited, never wavering

While I cleared old karma from my sin

As a man, a woman, a child, and other kin

Tragically, I never knew you existed

Until that day, I decided to stop speaking

Damn, my life was twisted

I was an empty vessel ready for the taking

I stopped eating, wanting nothing, hardly sleeping

You woke me up and started creeping

Up my spine

Rising higher, synovial fluid seeping

To my crown

Contracting and expanding with intensity

No heart beat now, my body is lighter—no density

Someone is rubbing the proverbial lamp with ghee

Is this the end? Genie, save me!

Personal Note and Reflections
Genie, Save Me!

My first Kundalini experience ignited a spiritual phenomenon known as samadhi—ultimate oneness with the Divine/God/Universe/Everlasting Light.

When my Spirit was released, I felt like the proverbial genie had escaped the lamp after being imprisoned for thousands of years.

I Am Night

I AM Night
You are Light
Ten million sunsets I have seen
Hues of purple, pink and tangerine
But nothing as beautiful as your glow
After we make love, I can see your halo
You pulled me out of darkness and melted my pain
You brought me joy and sunshine after the rain
Like a blanket, you wrapped around me with your wings
A loving whisper, a gentle kiss—oh, my heart sings
We spend a lifetime together without any words spoken
I thought I was bruised, battered and broken
But you showed me something deep inside
That was untouchable by mankind
My everlasting light from the Divine
I AM Light

Personal Note and Reflections
I Am Night

My realization, with angel guidance that there is a part of us that is untouchable by any event, interaction or experience on this physical plane. We are One with the Divine! We are Light.

New Heart

I felt safe hiding behind the numbers game
Studied math, accounting, architecture; it's all the same
I might say hello, but don't tell me your name
Can't get too close 'cause I might feel your pain
Brick by brick, I built a wall for protection
Avoided drama, avoided heartache, avoided rejection
Married with kids, yet I still kept my distance
I love them so much, yet there's always resistance

Until my heart suddenly stopped beating one night
My body lay still in bed, and my Spirit took flight
Angels worked on that body until Dawn's first light
Felt a kiss on my forehead; Spirit returned to my delight
Every cell of my being was now flooded with love
A New heart awakens—a gift from above

Personal Note and Reflections
New Heart

The first half of this poem is about avoiding my empathic and intuitive gifts. We can only put up so much resistance until our true nature gets our attention one way or another. That night my physical heart stopped beating, but my spiritual heart awoke.

Who This?

Went from wearing suits and heels, and carrying briefcases
To tank tops, yoga pants, and shoes with no laces
Ditched the mascara and chemical-laced perm
Make-up-free, twist braids became the norm
R&B, hip hop, soca and reggae are still sweet
Added chanting, drumming and singing bowls to the beat

Where are the cookies, ice cream and cereal, my kids asked
Try oatmeal, watercress, wild salmon or bass
Out went the microwave and cordless phones; cut the cable
TV-free, family meals twice a day at the kitchen table

Found my new groove in writing and public speaking
Heart and soul aligned whenever I did sound healing
Who this? I asked, staring in the mirror
The one who lives in heart now and forever

Personal Note and Reflections
Who This?

We evolve and transform through circumstances, finding our way on this life walk. Changes in personal frequency change our interests and values accordingly.

New Ears

I hear Mama looking for her newborn baby
I hear two lovers enjoying each other's company
I hear the leader of the pack
I hear prey eating a snack
I had never heard these sounds before
New ears listening to birds; I adore

I hear a beautiful rhythm, like a drum
Feet naked, hearing the ground hum
As I kiss the Earth with my feet
She responds with a melodic beat
I had never heard these sounds before
New ears listening to Mother Earth; I adore

I hear wheels spinning round and round
Some slow, some fast, cyclical sound
I hear the hollowness, yearning for more
I hear the loudness, the excess that is stored
I had never heard these sounds before
New ears listening to chakras; I adore

Personal Note and Reflections
New Ears

Many people who have been through an awakening often change in physical or energetic ways. When I awoke, I heard the world differently and connected to Nature, self and others in a much deeper way.

New Eyes

Music, sound, tempo and vibration

The piano was the subject of my adoration

I played for hours after school

Felt so nurtured, safe and cool

But these good feelings faded one August day

My first recital got me anxious, with stage fright at play

I lost it, vision gone, could not see a damn thing

Sitting at the piano, I heard the judge say, "Dawn, please begin."

My soul whispered to me, "Dawn, you don't need them to see."

I took a deep breath, placing both thumbs on middle C

I played my piece like I had done a hundred times before

Melting into the rhythm, the cadence, the score

I finished strong and won second place

However, the greatest prize was seeing my parent's face

When my vision returned after the event

I felt something new inside; I felt *confident*

As the years passed, my academic life excelled

Skipped three grades in nine years, I was compelled

To understand how far my confidence could extend
I got out of my comfort zone again and again
Conquering every phobia and fear until
All I see now is passion, purpose and Divine will
Believe in yourself; you are perfect in every way
Believe in yourself; new eyes revealed that August day

Personal Note and Reflections
New Eyes

At age nine, I lost my vision at my very first piano recital. An unforgettable day!

I also gained something that day which spilled over into my school life and eventually my career life—confidence!

Unseen World

Light, frequency and sound
Ley lines in the ground

Aura, chakras and meridian
Swami, Dogon and Dravidian

Angels and channelers joined my tribe
Essential oils and crystals raised my vibe

Monthly water fasts to cleanse my being
Purify my cells, unleashed energy streaming

Through every atom from head to toe
Connected to my soul star above a halo

Divine love and spiritual wisdom inhaled
I surrender to the unseen world—*unveiled*.

Personal Note and Reflections
Unseen World

The higher you raise your frequency, the more you can perceive subtle energies—even feel your aura. Purifying the body of toxins is part of maintaining a high frequency.

Freedom

The greatest freedom is to want nothing from this physical plane

Not money, not sex, not food, not material gain

Stress begins when we create inner tension

From thoughts and feelings of dissatisfaction

Illusions of feeling incomplete

Creating cravings, then we deplete

Our innate intelligence fades into the background

So, you ask, how do we turn this around?

By remembering the wonderful talents and gifts you possess

You learned 500 things before starting school or having a recess

You are a brilliant spiritual being with endless potential

Tune into the Universe and your heart for riches, exponential

Personal Note and Reflections
Freedom

I became detached from the physical world during a three-month period when I ate virtually no food.

I wanted nothing. It was a whole new level of freedom.

My new mantra became All I Need is Within Me.

We want nothing when we remember we have everything we need.

Your Reflections

Other Works By Dawn

The Trilogy available at www.RaiseTheVibration.ca

Raise Your Vibration, Transform Your Life

(English, Spanish)

How to Raise the Vibration Around You

Raise the Vibration Between Us

(English, Spanish, French)

Raise the Vibration Between Us (audiobook)

https://dawnjames.ca/raise-the-vibration-between-us-audio/

Why Are We Here (audiobook)

https://dawnjames.ca/why-are-we-here/

Unveiled: Autobiography of an Awakened One

https://dawnjames.ca/unveiled

New Eyes: Awakened Poems (audiobook & fillable PDF)

https://dawnjames.ca/neweyes

About Dawn

Dawn James is a bestselling and award-winning author for her unforgettable afterlife story, *UNVEILED: Autobiography of an Awakened One* (2022 Silver Award for Nonfiction/ Spirituality; Readers' Favorite).

In *UNVEILED*, Dawn shares her incredible life and spiritual journey and strengthens her connection to a higher power, which was partly inspired by the health challenges and physical phenomena she faced as a child, including deafness, blindness, and paralysis. Several spiritual concepts are explained in *UNVEILED*, including Kundalini awakening, Merkabah, Breatharians, Unity Consciousness, Soul Mates, and Harmonic Concordance, to name a few.

Inspired to start writing by some encouraging words from the late Sylvia Browne, Dawn published the *Raise Your Vibration* trilogy, which teaches others to live mindfully and in harmony with each other and the planet.

Read her Trilogy in this order:

Book 1: Raise Your Vibration, Transform Your Life

Book 2: How to Raise the Vibration around You

Book 3: Raise the Vibration Between Us

SHE LIVED, SHE DIED, SHE AWAKENED

After a spiritual awakening and a series of spiritual events in 2003, Dawn became a writer and sound healer. Since her "wake-up" call, she has dedicated her life to teaching others how to raise their awareness and understand and improve their personal vibrational frequency for overall health and wellness. Today, she shares her knowledge of healthy living, healing, and spiritual growth through her transformational books and tropical retreats.

Connect With Dawn

Learn more about her heart work, soul work and sound work at **https://DawnJames.ca**

Join Dawn for a soulful experience at **www.SoulfulHealingRetreats.com**

Ready to share your story? Visit **www.TheRightPlacetoWrite.com**

Youtube: Subscribe here
https://youtube.com/raiseyourvibr8n

Blog: For high-vibe inspiration and wellness tips
https://DawnJames.ca/blog

Soulful Tribe Newsletter
https://bit.ly/soultribedj

Writers' Community Newsletter
https://bit.ly/writersrus

www.ingramcontent.com/pod-product-compliance
Lightning Source LLC
Chambersburg PA
CBHW021952160426
43209CB00001B/10